P9-CFE-410

DATE DUE

2011

WHY WE WON
THE
AMERICAN REVOLUTION—
THROUGH
PRIMARY SOURCES

John Micklos, Jr.

Enslow Publishers, Inc.
40 Industrial Road
Box 398
Berkeley Heights, NJ 07922
USA
http://www.enslow.com

Original edition published as *How the Revolutionary War Was Won* in 2008.

Library of Congress Cataloging-in-Publication Data

Micklos, John.
  [How the Revolutionary War Was Won]
  Why we won the American Revolution—through primary sources / John Micklos, Jr.
      p. cm. — (The American Revolution through primary sources)
  "Original edition published as How the Revolutionary War Was Won in 2008."
  Includes bibliographical references and index.
  Summary: "Examines how and why the United States defeated Great Britain in the American Revolution, including the
    key turning points, the significant battles, and the important leaders"—Provided by publisher.
  ISBN 978-0-7660-4134-9
  1. United States—History—Revolution, 1775–1783—Campaigns—Juvenile literature. 2. United States—History—
  Revolution, 1775–1783—Naval operations—Juvenile literature. 3. United States. Continental Army—History—Juvenile
  literature. 4. United States. Navy—History—Revolution, 1775–1783—Juvenile literature. 5. Great Britain. Army—
  History—18th century—Juvenile literature. 6. Great Britain. Royal Navy—History—18th century—Juvenile literature.
  7. Soldiers—United States—History—18th century—Juvenile literature. 8. Sailors—United States—History—18th
  century—Juvenile literature. 9. Spies—United States—History—18th century—Juvenile literature. I. Title.
  E230.M46 2013
  973.3'3—dc23
                              2012015700
Future editions:
Paperback ISBN 978-1-4644-0192-3
ePUB ISBN 978-1-4645-1105-9
PDF ISBN 978-1-4646-1105-6

Printed in the United States of America
082012 Lake Book Manufacturing, Inc., Melrose Park, IL

10 9 8 7 6 5 4 3 2 1

To Our Readers: We have done our best to make sure all Internet Addresses in this book were active and appropriate when we went to press. However, the author and the publisher have no control over and assume no liability for the material available on those Internet sites or on other Web sites they may link to. Any comments or suggestions can be sent by email to comments@enslow.com or to the address on the back cover.

♻ Enslow Publishers, Inc., is committed to printing our books on recycled paper. The paper in every book contains 10% to 30% post-consumer waste (PCW). The cover board on the outside of each book contains 100% PCW. Our goal is to do our part to help young people and the environment too!

Illustration Credits: © Corel Corporation, p. 40; Domenick D'Andrea, courtesy of the National Guard, pp. 1, 3, 4–5, 13, 21, 25, 31; Library of Congress Manuscript Division, pp. 11, 14; Library of Congress Prints and Photographs, pp. 17, 20, 23, 24, 28, 30; National Archives, p. 9; U.S. Army Center of Military History, p. 37; U.S. Senate Collection, p. 18; Valley Forge National Historic Park, pp. 7, 32; Vault Collection, North Carolina State Archives, p. 26.

Cover Illustration: Domenick D'Andrea, courtesy of the National Guard (Illustration depicts soldiers in the Continental Army firing their muskets at the Battle of Long Island).

CONTENTS

LOOK FOR THIS SYMBOL **PRIMARY SOURCE** TO FIND THE PRIMARY SOURCES THROUGHOUT THIS BOOK.

Continental Army troops fire their muskets during the Battle of Long Island.

CHAPTER 1

⭐

REBELS AND REDCOATS

On the morning of August 22, 1776, five large ships dropped anchor off the southwestern coast of Long Island, New York. The ships all flew the flag of Britain's Royal Navy. And they all had big cannons ready to blast the shoreline if necessary. Soon dozens of flatboats filled the narrow waters between Long Island and Staten Island to the west. The boats were crammed with British soldiers. Sailors rowed the boats to a beach at Gravesend Bay. At eight o'clock, the soldiers went ashore.

They presented an impressive sight. There were 4,000 men in all. But it did not take long for them to form orderly ranks.

The soldiers' uniforms included red coats. The polished brass buttons on these coats gleamed in the sunlight. So did the soldiers' bayonets—long steel blades attached to the ends of their muskets.

Meanwhile, the flatboats returned to Staten Island to pick up more soldiers. By midday, a massive force of 15,000 men occupied southwestern Long Island. Regiments—large units made up of hundreds of soldiers—were gathered in precise formation on the plain there.

Moving and organizing so many men in such a short time was not easy. It required good officers and well-trained men. The British Army had both. It was perhaps the best army in the world.

The army was a career for most British soldiers, who were known as redcoats. Men who enlisted during peacetime agreed to serve for life. Men recruited during wartime had to serve for three years or until the war was over. The redcoats on Long Island had a lot of military experience. On average, these men had been in the army for nearly six years.[1] The British soldiers were tough and proud. They were confident of their fighting skills.

PRIMARY SOURCE

The musket and bayonet were essential weapons during the American Revolution. This photo shows two American muskets along with a bayonet.

The British soldiers had little respect for the men they had been sent to Long Island to fight. Unlike the redcoats, these men were not professional soldiers. Most had a year or less of military experience. They were ordinary people from all walks of life: farmers, storekeepers, and tradesmen. However, most important from the British point of view, they were rebels.

In July 1776, the thirteen American colonies had officially broken away from Britain. Meeting in Philadelphia, representatives of the colonies—the Continental Congress—issued the Declaration of Independence. It listed the ways Britain's King George III had violated the colonists' rights. It said that the Americans were no longer subjects of the king. They were citizens of the free and independent United States.

By the time the Declaration was issued, the American Revolution had been going on for more than a year. The fighting began on April 19, 1775. That day, a large force of redcoats fought against Massachusetts militia units. The militias were groups of American colonists from the same town or area. They were not full-time soldiers. They were private citizens who trained together and agreed to turn out with their weapons in an emergency. The redcoats had marched out of Boston, where they were headquartered. They planned to seize weapons and supplies the colonists had hidden. At the villages of Lexington and Concord,

The Declaration of Independence, signed July 4, 1776, stated the American colonists were no longer subjects of King George III, but free fighting broke out. Throughout the redcoats' long march back to Boston, militiamen shot at them.

After the battles at Lexington and Concord, about twenty thousand American men flocked to the area around Boston. Many came from Massachusetts. But many were from the other New England colonies. These men took up positions outside Boston. They called themselves the "Army of Observation." Really, though, they were more like a collection of militia groups than an army. There was no overall commander. Each colony considered its militia an independent force.

Most British officers thought little of the Americans. One general, John Burgoyne, called them an "untrained rabble."[2] They would never be able to stand up to the mighty British army, Burgoyne said. Yet for weeks, the Army of Observation kept British soldiers trapped inside Boston.

On June 17, the British finally came out of the city. In a bloody battle fought on Bunker Hill and nearby Breed's Hill, they found that the "rabble" would stand up and fight.

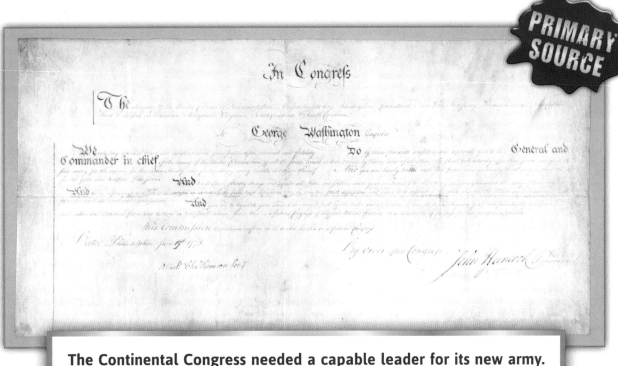

The Continental Congress needed a capable leader for its new army. This document, signed at the bottom by John Hancock, declared George Washington general and commander-in-chief of the Continental Army.

At the time, there were only about 8,000 redcoats in America. British leaders realized they would need a lot more soldiers to stamp out the rebellion. Regiment after regiment was sent from England to America. King George also hired thousands of German professional soldiers. These soldiers were known as Hessians.

Leaders in the Continental Congress also realized it would take more than militia to fight the British. A regular army was needed. In June 1775, Congress created the Continental Army and appointed George Washington of Virginia as its commander. The new Continental Army would be formed from the so-called Army of Observation outside Boston. Each colony would also raise additional regiments.

In early July, Washington arrived in Massachusetts to take command of the army. He was shocked by what he saw. The troops did not look or act like disciplined soldiers. Drunkenness and brawling were common. Men seemed to wander in and out of camp as they pleased. Also, food and supplies were scarce.

Washington did his best to bring order to his army. But he feared that the British might launch a full-scale attack. He was not sure his men could stop it.

Yet the British did not attack. For months, the siege of Boston continued. Finally, on March 17, 1776, the redcoats left the city aboard British ships.

Washington marched most of his men south to New York City. He expected the British to attack there. It would be the first big test for the Continental Army.

CHAPTER 2

★

AMERICAN ARMY
ON THE RUN

Defending New York City presented quite a challenge for George Washington. The city was located on the southern tip of Manhattan Island. And the Royal Navy controlled the surrounding waters. During the spring and summer of 1776, a huge British fleet arrived in the area. It included thirty heavily-armed warships and about four hundred transport ships.[1] Washington had no navy.

Washington decided to protect New York City by fortifying Brooklyn Heights. This high ground was on Long Island. It was less than a half mile across the East River from Manhattan. From Brooklyn, the American positions extended east across a series of wooded hills known as the Heights of Guan.

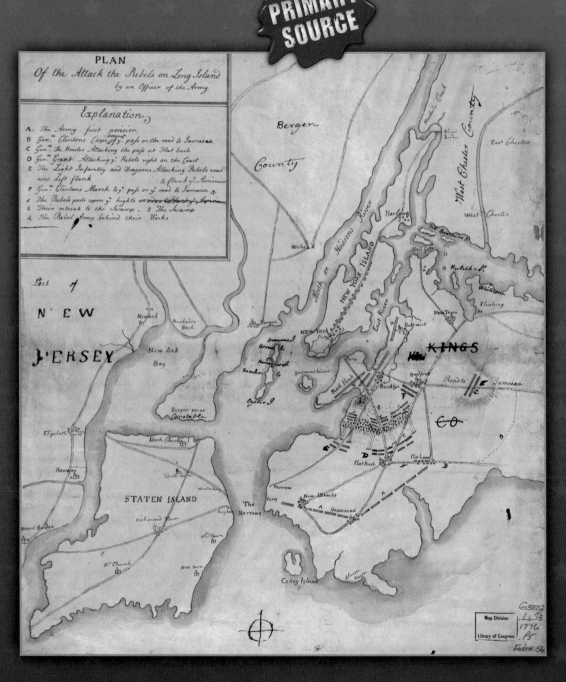

This 1776 map shows the British attack plan against the Continental Army on Long Island. It also details Staten Island, New York Island (present-day Manhattan), and other parts of New York and New Jersey.

By the middle of August, the British had 32,000 men on Staten Island. These included 8,000 Hessians.[2] General William Howe, the British commander, ordered 20,000 of his troops to Long Island. They began landing on August 22.

George Washington had as many as 23,000 men under his command.[3] But almost half of these men were sick. Also, many of Washington's troops were militiamen rather than Continental Army regulars. Very few of the Continentals had experience in battle. They were poorly equipped. But at least they had a bit more training than the militia. Still, no one knew how the Continentals or the militia would perform in a pitched battle.

The answer came on the morning of August 27. The night before, thousands of redcoats had swung around the left side of the American lines. The Americans had failed to guard a pass through the Heights of Guan. Around 9 A.M., redcoats attacked the Americans from behind. British and Hessian troops charged from the front. The left and center of the American lines collapsed.

Terrified Continental regulars and militiamen abandoned their positions and fled for their lives.

"It is impossible for me to describe the confusion and horror of the scene," recalled Michael Graham, an eighteen-year-old soldier from Pennsylvania. Americans, Graham said, were "running in almost every direction, and run which way they would, they were almost sure to meet the British or Hessians."[4] Some of these fleeing Americans were taken prisoner. But many were bayoneted.

By noon, the Battle of Long Island was over. The American soldiers had been beaten badly. Of about 10,000 Americans who had fought in the battle, more than 1,400 were killed, wounded, or captured. Combined, the British and Hessians suffered fewer than four hundred casualties.[5]

If General Howe had moved quickly, he might have been able to trap Washington and more than 9,000 American soldiers on Brooklyn Heights. But Howe delayed. On the night of August 29–30, Washington and his men escaped to New York City on small boats.

By the fall of 1776, British troops had gained control of New York. In this illustration made in the 1770s, British redcoats parade through the streets of New York City.

It was not long before the British attacked again. Supported by the big guns of Royal Navy warships anchored in the East River, redcoats landed north of New York City on September 15. The Connecticut militiamen who were supposed to hold the area simply ran away. Seeing this, George Washington roared, "Are these the men with which I am to defend America?"[6]

The British soon controlled New York City. They would hold it for the rest of the war.

Charles Willson Peale painted this portrait of George Washington in 1779. Although the British had soundly beaten the Continental Army in the early part of the war, General Washington did not give up and planned a daring attack in December 1776.

PRIMARY SOURCE

Meanwhile, Washington changed his strategy. He realized that with the army he had, he could not win the war by engaging the British in a single large battle. He would have to fight a defensive war. At all costs, he would have to keep his army intact and in the field. In this way, he hoped to wear down the British until they got tired of fighting.

However, during the final months of 1776, it seemed doubtful that Washington would be able to keep an army in the field.

The British chased the retreating Americans up Manhattan Island, across the Hudson River, and through New Jersey. Finally, on December 11, Washington's weary soldiers escaped across the Delaware River into Pennsylvania.

But the army was in tatters. Militiamen had gone home by the thousands. Many Continental Army soldiers had deserted. Washington's force now consisted of fewer than 2,500 men. And the enlistments of most of these soldiers were set to expire at the end of the year. At that time, the Continental Army might simply fade away. The American Revolution would be over.

Washington was not ready to let that happen. On Christmas night, he again led his ragged troops across the Delaware River. The following morning, the Americans attacked the British in Trenton, New Jersey. Washington's men surprised and routed the Hessian force occupying the town. More than one hundred of the German professional soldiers were killed or wounded in the fierce hour-long battle, while another nine hundred surrendered. Only four Americans were wounded.

George Washington stands with a group of soldiers as they look at the captured British flags after the American victory in the Battle of Trenton.

A week later, Washington struck again, and his troops defeated the British at Princeton, New Jersey.

These two victories gave new hope to the American cause. Many soldiers extended their enlistment. The Continental Army remained intact.

CHAPTER 3

★

SNEAKY SPIES AND TRICKY TRAITORS

George Washington's surprise attack on Trenton in December 1776 was extremely daring. Many things could have gone wrong. But at least Washington had taken an important step to increase his odds of success: he had found a person to spy on the British.

John Honeyman lived a few miles from Trenton. A cattle dealer, he supplied British and Hessian troops with meat and moved freely about their camps. Years earlier, Honeyman had served in the British army, and he publicly proclaimed his loyalty to the king. Secretly, however, he supported the American side.

On December 22, Honeyman allowed himself to be captured by an American patrol as he walked near the banks of the Delaware.

He was taken to Washington's headquarters. There, Honeyman described in great detail the Hessian forces in Trenton, including where their sentries were posted.[1] Armed with this information, Washington planned his attack.

Washington keenly understood the value of spies. So did the British. Spies could gather and pass information about enemy troop movements or battle plans. They might even be used to spread false information, tricking the enemy.

During the American Revolution, the number of Americans who favored independence (people who called themselves patriots) was about the same as the number who remained loyal to the king (called loyalists). For this reason, neither side had too much difficulty recruiting spies.

Men, women, and even children served as spies. Sometimes their work was as simple as sitting in a tavern and listening to an important piece of information from an enemy soldier. Other times it required sneaking behind enemy lines. Spies knew that if they were captured, they would probably be hanged.

During the American Revolution, a few people switched their allegiance (loyalty) from one side to the other. The most famous of these traitors was the American general Benedict Arnold.

Upset that he had been passed over for Continental Army promotions, Arnold offered to turn West Point over to the British. This was a key fort on the Hudson River north of New York City. In September 1780, after exchanging a series of letters with the

During the American Revolution, women proved to be valuable spies. In this illustration, Lydia Darragh gives reports on British troop movements to one of General Washington's colonels.

PRIMARY SOURCE

The infamous traitor Benedict Arnold is shown here in a portrait from 1776. After the failed West Point plot, Arnold escaped capture and served as a British general until the war ended.

British, Arnold met secretly with the British agent John André. As André made his way back to British lines, however, he was captured. The West Point plot was discovered, and André was hanged as a spy. Arnold was luckier. He managed to escape. He served as a British general until the end of the war.

★

CHAPTER 4

THE WAR AT SEA

Britain had the world's strongest navy. At the beginning of the American Revolution, the Royal Navy included some 270 warships. Nearly two hundred more warships would be added before the war was over. The Americans, on the other hand, started the war without a single warship. Congress established the Continental navy in late 1775. But the navy was always relatively small. It never seriously challenged Britain's control of the seas.

This gave the British many advantages. In battles fought along the coast or near large rivers, Royal Navy ships were able to support British soldiers by bombarding American troops. The British also

IN CONGRESS.

The DELEGATES of the UNITED COLONIES of *New-Hampshire, Massachusetts-Bay, Rhode-Island, Connecticut, New-York, New-Jersey, Pennsylvania,* the Counties of *New-Castle, Kent* and *Suffex* on *Delaware, Maryland, Virginia, North-Carolina, South-Carolina,* and *Georgia,* TO All unto whom these Presents shall come, send GREETING: KNOW YE,

THAT we have granted, and by these Presents do grant Licence and Authority to *James Powel* — Mariner, Commander of the *schooner* called *the Northampton* of the Burthen of *thirty* Tons, or thereabouts, belonging to *John Harmanson & Com* — of *Northampton* in the Colony of *Virginia* mounting *four* Carriage Guns, and navigated by *thirty* Men, to fit out and set forth the said *schooner* in a warlike Manner, and by and with the said *Powel* and the Crew thereof, by Force of Arms, to attack, seize, and take the Ships and other Vessels belonging to the Inhabitants of Great-Britain, or any of them, with their Tackle, Apparel, Furniture and Ladings, on the High Seas, or between high-water and low-water Marks, and to bring the same to some convenient Ports in the said Colonies, in Order that the Courts, which are or shall be there appointed to hear and determine Causes civil and maritime, may proceed in due Form to condemn the said Captures, if they be adjudged lawful Prize; the said *James Powel* having given Bond, with sufficient Sureties, that Nothing be done by the said *James Powel* or any of the Officers, Mariners or Company thereof contrary to, or inconsistent with the Usages and Customs of Nations, and the Instructions, a Copy of which is herewith delivered to him. And we will and require all our Officers whatsoever to give Succour and Assistance to the said *James Powel* in the Premises. This Commission shall continue in Force until the Congress shall issue Orders to the Contrary. *By Order of the Congress,*

Dated at *Virginia October 24th 1776*

John Hancock PRESIDENT.

The Continental Congress issued this Letter of Marque, signed by John Hancock, on October 24, 1776, to a ship captain named James Powell. This type of letter gave American privateers official permission to attack and seize British ships.

used their fleet to transport soldiers and equipment. On several campaigns, large British armies were moved long distances by the Royal Navy. Continental soldiers, by contrast, had to march. And if a British force got trapped, it could be evacuated by sea.

The Royal Navy may have ruled the seas, but the Americans were still determined to strike at British shipping. To do this, they relied heavily on privateers. Privateers were ships—usually merchant vessels—that had been outfitted with some cannons. They were privately owned and operated. The owner of a privateer obtained from the Continental Congress a document called a

Dangerous Work

During the American Revolution, a total of fifty-seven ships served in the Continental navy for some period.[1] Nearly two-thirds of these ships were sunk, destroyed, captured, or lost at sea.

This period illustration shows the naval battle between the _Bonhomme Richard_ and the _Serapis_.

Letter of Marque. This gave the privateer authority to attack and seize any British ship.

When a privateer captured an enemy vessel, that vessel and its cargo were sold. The owner of the privateer and its crew split the profits. The American government also received a share.

During the eight years of the American Revolution, more than 1,100 American privateer ships roamed the seas. The Royal Navy

Naval Hero

Scottish-born John Paul Jones ranks as America's most famous naval hero of the American Revolution. Jones was commissioned an officer in the Continental navy in December 1775. Over the following years, he captured or sank dozens of British ships. In 1778, he even raided the English port of Whitehaven. It was the only time during the American Revolution that American rebels attacked on English soil. The British public was outraged. "Where is the British navy?" asked the newspapers.[2]

Jones is best remembered, however, for a 1779 sea battle off the eastern coast of England. He rammed his seriously outgunned ship *Bonhomme Richard* into the British warship *Serapis*. With Jones's vessel taking heavy fire and filling with water, the captain of the *Serapis* asked if he wished to surrender. "I have not yet begun to fight," Jones replied.[3] After hours of close combat, it was the captain of the *Serapis* who surrendered. Badly damaged, the *Bonhomme Richard* later sank.

PRIMARY SOURCE

John Paul Jones, America's greatest naval hero during the Revolution, is shown in this Charles Willson Peale portrait from 1781.

sank or seized many of these ships, killing or capturing many American sailors. But privateers did capture more than six hundred British merchant ships.[4] In so doing, they obtained much-needed supplies for the Continental Army.

Overall, though, American privateers—like the Continental Navy—were little more than an annoyance to the Royal Navy. Britain's control of the seas was threatened only when France joined the United States as an ally. And in the end, French naval power would play a key role in deciding the outcome of the war.

CHAPTER 5

★

THE AMERICANS FIGHT ON... AND WIN!

In 1777, the British mounted two major campaigns. In June, more than 7,000 soldiers under the command of General John Burgoyne invaded northern New York from Canada. In late August, General William Howe landed 15,000 redcoats and Hessians in the northern Chesapeake Bay and marched them northeast toward Philadelphia.

Burgoyne's invasion ended badly for the British. American forces wore down Burgoyne's army. On October 17, after the Battle of Saratoga, Burgoyne surrendered.

General Howe had more luck. On September 11, his troops defeated Washington's army at Brandywine Creek, Pennsylvania.

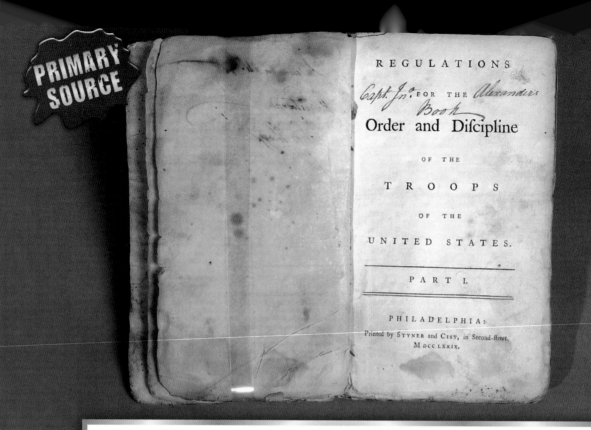

REGULATIONS

Capt. Jn.º FOR THE *Alexander's Book*

Order and Difcipline

OF THE

T R O O P S

OF THE

U N I T E D   S T A T E S.

P A R T   I.

PHILADELPHIA:

Printed by STYNER and CIST, in Second-ftreet.
M DCC LXXIX.

Friedrich von Steuben helped George Washington train the American troops during their winter at Valley Forge. This photo shows pages from von Steuben's training manual called *Regulations for the Order and Discipline of the Troops of the United States*.

Two weeks later, the British marched into Philadelphia, forcing the Continental Congress to flee the city.

Washington tried to strike back. On October 4, his troops attacked redcoats and Hessians camped a few miles north of Philadelphia, in the village of Germantown. The Continentals surprised the enemy, but they were eventually forced to retreat.

Washington decided to camp for the winter at Valley Forge, about twenty-five miles away.

The Continental Army spent the winter of 1777–1778 huddled in crude wooden huts at Valley Forge. Washington's army suffered terrible hardships. Many men did not have winter coats. Many did not even have shoes. Food, too, was scarce. Under the difficult winter conditions at Valley Forge, about 2,500 of the 10,000 soldiers died.

Still, the Continental Army came out of Valley Forge stronger. Much of the credit belongs to Friedrich von Steuben. He was an experienced officer from the German kingdom of Prussia. Von Steuben volunteered to train Washington's army in European methods of fighting. He taught Continental units to move and maneuver effectively on the battlefield.

The value of this training became clear at Monmouth Court House in New Jersey. The British had abandoned Philadelphia and were on the march to New York City. Washington decided to attack them on June 28, 1778. The fighting was fierce.

Alliance With France

Even though the Americans lost at Germantown, the battle was important for the patriot cause. The battle showed French leaders that George Washington was not going to give up. The American victory at Saratoga convinced the French that the Americans could win.

England was a longtime enemy of France. The French had secretly been providing money and supplies to the Americans. But French leaders did not want to commit soldiers and ships to a lost cause. The events in the autumn of 1777 helped persuade France to sign a treaty of alliance with the United States early the following year.

But the Continentals held their own in a full-scale battle. Clearly, Washington's army had improved.

Monmouth was the last major battle fought in the northern colonies. The British kept most of their troops in New York City, which meant that Washington had to keep the main part of the

Continental Army nearby. But large British forces sailed out to conquer the South.

In December 1778, the British captured Savannah, Georgia, an important port city. In May 1780, after a long siege, they took Charleston, South Carolina's capital. And on August 16, 1780, the Americans suffered an even more severe blow at Camden, South Carolina. There, British general Lord Charles Cornwallis smashed the Continental Army in the South, which was commanded by General Horatio Gates. More than 2,000 Americans were wounded, killed, or captured in the battle.

In December 1780, Nathanael Greene took command of what was left of the Continental Army in the South. General Greene lured Cornwallis into chasing his ragged force. During the first months of 1781, the redcoats pursued Greene's army all the way through North Carolina. It was rugged country, and Cornwallis's army ran low on food and supplies.

On March 14, the two armies finally met at Guilford Courthouse, North Carolina. More than one-quarter of General

Cornwallis's men were killed or wounded in the battle. The British general decided to abandon the Carolinas and move into Virginia. His army eventually settled in Yorktown, a port on the York River. Ships could reach it by sailing up the Chesapeake Bay. Cornwallis chose the location because he believed that it would allow his troops to be reinforced or evacuated by the Royal Navy.

During the summer, a French army commanded by the Comte de Rochambeau joined Washington's army north of New York City. In August, Rochambeau and Washington received word that the French admiral Comte de Grasse was sailing a large fleet of warships to the Chesapeake Bay. Washington and Rochambeau decided to attack Cornwallis at Yorktown.

Washington took steps to make it seem that he was preparing to attack New York City. British spies reported this to General Henry Clinton, the British commander in chief. In reality, 2,500 Continentals under Washington's command began a rapid march toward Yorktown on August 17. They were joined by more than 4,000 French troops under Rochambeau.

Continental Army soldiers stand ready for a British attack during the Battle at Guilford Courthouse in North Carolina.

By early September, when the French and American soldiers reached Philadelphia, Clinton realized what was happening. He wrote to warn Cornwallis. But de Grasse's fleet had already arrived in the Chesapeake. Hundreds of French troops went ashore. They joined 2,500 Continentals who were already hemming the British in at Yorktown.

On September 5, a British fleet, commanded by Admiral Thomas Graves, arrived near the mouth of the Chesapeake. De Grasse's French warships sailed out to meet the British. In the Battle of the Virginia Capes, de Grasse battered the English fleet. Graves decided to take his ships to New York.

Without the Royal Navy to help him, Cornwallis was in danger. But he expected Clinton to send more ships and reinforcements.

In New York, some British generals urged Clinton to do just that. "Destruction of the whole is certain if the army in Virginia is destroyed," said one.[1] Yet Clinton delayed. He could not decide what to do.

By late September, the combined forces of Washington and Rochambeau had completed their long trip from New York. Militia from Virginia and Maryland also arrived, bringing the total number of American soldiers around Yorktown to about 9,000. A similar number of French troops were present. And another French fleet, commanded by Admiral de Barras, had arrived. It brought siege guns. These were heavy cannons that could destroy the fortifications Cornwallis's men had erected around Yorktown.

On the night of October 6, American and French troops dug trenches in which to place the siege guns. Three days later, the big guns opened fire, hurling cannonballs and exploding shells into Yorktown. For the next several days, the cannons fired constantly. Meanwhile, the French and Americans extended their trenches closer and closer to the British lines.

On the night of October 16, Cornwallis tried to move his troops across the York River to Gloucester Point, where there was a small British force. From there, he hoped to break through the enemy lines and escape. A sudden storm stopped the attempt. The situation for the British was now hopeless.

Freedom's Fallen

An estimated 200,000 Americans served in the Continental Army or a state militia at some time during the Revolution. It is impossible to know exactly how many died during their service. An estimate by scholars at the University of Michigan puts the number at more than 25,000. Of these, an estimated 6,284 were killed in action, 10,000 died in camp from disease, and 8,500 more died as prisoners.[2] The number of dead was almost 1 percent of the total population of the American colonies at the time.[3]

In this John Trumbull painting, Cornwallis's officers surrender to the Continental Army after the American victory at Yorktown.

On October 17, a British officer standing on a fortification waved a white handkerchief. This signaled Cornwallis's decision to discuss terms of surrender. Two days later, on October 19, the 8,000 men under Cornwallis's command marched out of Yorktown to lay down their arms.

Yorktown marked the last major battle of the American Revolution. Though a peace treaty would take two long years to hammer out, British leaders recognized that they could no longer hope to win the war. The United States had won independence.

TIMELINE

1775

On April 19, the American Revolution begins with the battles of Lexington and Concord.

On June 17, the British win a costly victory at the Battle of Bunker Hill, outside Boston.

In early July, George Washington takes command of the Continental Army.

An American attempt to capture Quebec on December 31 fails.

1776

The British evacuate Boston on March 17.

On July 4, the Continental Congress issues the Declaration of Independence.

Washington's army is routed at the Battle of Long Island, August 27.

On September 15, the British land on Manhattan Island. The Continental Army soon abandons New York City.

American spy Nathan Hale is hanged in New York on September 22.

On December 26, Washington's army captures the Hessian outpost at Trenton, New Jersey.

1777

On January 3, Washington wins another battle at Princeton, New Jersey.

The British defeat American troops at the Battle of Brandywine on September 11. They soon capture Philadelphia.

The British turn back an American assault at Germantown on October 4.

On October 17, British general John Burgoyne surrenders his army to American general Horatio Gates in Saratoga, New York.

1778

France signs a treaty of alliance with the United States and declares war on England.

On June 28, American and British troops fight a fierce, daylong battle at Monmouth Court House, New Jersey.

At its winter camp in Valley Forge, the Continental Army receives valuable training from Friedrich von Steuben.

In December, the British capture Savannah, Georgia.

1779

In September, John Paul Jones wins a sea battle off the coast of England. He becomes the patriots' first naval hero.

American general Benedict Arnold begins giving military secrets to the British.

In September and October, a patriot effort to recapture Savannah fails.

1780

On May 12, the British capture Charleston, South Carolina.

On August 16, a British army under the command of Lord Cornwallis smashes the Continental Army in the South at the Battle of Camden, South Carolina.

Benedict Arnold's plot to turn over control of West Point is discovered in late September.

American militiamen win a battle at King's Mountain in South Carolina on October 7.

In December, Nathanael Greene takes command of the Continental Army in the South.

1781–1783

On March 15, 1781, Greene cripples Cornwallis's army at the Battle of Guilford Courthouse in North Carolina. Cornwallis gives up his plan to conquer the Carolinas and marches his troops into Virginia.

On August 17, 1781, a Continental force under the command of George Washington and a French force under the command of the Comte de Rochambeau begin a rapid march toward Yorktown, Virginia. Their plan is to trap Cornwallis's army there.

In the Battle of the Virginia Capes, fought on September 5, 1781, a French fleet defeats a British fleet near the mouth of the Chesapeake Bay.

In late September 1781, the armies of Washington and Rochambeau arrive outside Yorktown and lay siege to the town.

On October 19, 1781, Cornwallis surrenders at Yorktown.

On September 3, 1783, the Treaty of Paris is signed. This officially ends the war.

CHAPTER NOTES

CHAPTER 1: REBELS AND REDCOATS

1. David McCullough, *1776* (New York: Simon & Schuster, 2005), p. 167.
2. Gordon S. Wood, *The American Revolution* (New York: Modern Library, 2002), p. 54.

CHAPTER 2: AMERICAN ARMY ON THE RUN

1. Thomas Fleming, *Liberty! The American Revolution* (New York: Viking, 1997), p. 186.
2. Robert Middlekauff, *The Glorious Cause: The American Revolution, 1763–1789* (New York: Oxford University Press, 1982), p. 340.
3. Fleming, p. 181.
4. George DeWan, "The Patriots' First Big Test," *Newsday.com,* 2007, <http://www.newsday.com/community/guide/lihistory/ny-history-hs403a,0,6043581.story> (October 1, 2007).
5. Fleming, p. 194.
6. Ibid., p. 201.

CHAPTER 3: SNEAKY SPIES AND TRICKY TRAITORS

1. Thomas Fleming, *Liberty! The American Revolution* (New York: Viking, 1997), p. 214.

CHAPTER 4: THE WAR AT SEA

1. "Vessels of the Continental Navy," *U.S. Naval Historical Center,* February 6, 2002, <http://www.history.navy.mil/wars/revwar/contships.htm> (October 1, 2007).

2. Thomas Fleming, *Liberty! The American Revolution* (New York: Viking, 1997), p. 293.

3. Robert Middlekauff, *The Glorious Cause: The American Revolution, 1763–1789* (New York: Oxford University Press, 1982), p. 533.

4. Fleming, p. 298.

CHAPTER 5: THE AMERICANS FIGHT ON . . . AND WIN!

1. Richard M. Ketchum, *Victory at Yorktown: The Campaign That Won the Revolution* (New York: Henry Holt, 2004), p. 206.

2. Thomas Fleming, *Liberty! The American Revolution* (New York: Viking, 1997), p. 334.

3. David McCullough, *1776* (New York: Simon & Schuster, 2005), p. 294.

GLOSSARY

---☆---

allegiance—Loyalty to a person, group, or cause.

alliance—A formal agreement between countries to work together.

campaign—A connected series of military operations that form a particular phase of a war.

enlistment—The act of signing up for military service; the period of time for which a soldier agrees to serve.

evacuate—To remove from a dangerous area.

fortifications—Defensive structures, such as forts, walls, and barricades.

militia—A group of private citizens who occasionally train together for military service and agree to serve in an emergency.

primary source—A document, text, or physical object which was written or created during the time under discussion.

privateer—A private ship licensed by the government to attack and capture enemy ships during wartime.

rabble—A mob; a disorderly crowd.

redcoat—A British soldier.

regular—A soldier who is a member of an official, organized army (as opposed to a militia).

reinforcements—An additional supply of troops.

siege—A military blockade of a city or fortified position, in order to force its defenders to surrender.

traitor—One who betrays his or her country.

FURTHER READING

Books

Fleming, Thomas. ***Everybody's Revolution: A New Look at the People Who Won America's Freedom.*** New York: Scholastic Nonfiction, 2006.

Freedman, Russell. ***Washington at Valley Forge.*** New York: Holiday House, 2008.

Huey, Lois Miner. ***Voices of the American Revolution: Stories From the Battlefields.*** Mankato, Minn.: Capstone Press, 2011.

Marston, Daniel. ***The American Revolutionary War.*** New York: Rosen Publishing Group, 2011.

Roberts, Russell. ***The Battle of Yorktown.*** Hockessin, Del.: Mitchell Lane Publishers, 2011.

Internet Addresses

PBS—Liberty!: The American Revolution
<http://www.pbs.org/ktca/liberty/>

Yorktown National Battlefield
<http://www.nps.gov/yonb/index.htm>

INDEX